LEGENDS OF WARFARE

AVIATION

F-22 Raptor

Lockheed Martin Stealth Fighter

KEN NEUBECK

SCHIFFER MILITARY

4880 Lower Valley Road · Atglen, PA 19310

Designed by Christopher Bower
Cover design by Christopher Bower
Type set in Impact/Minion Pro

ISBN: 978-0-7643-6791-5
Printed in India

Published by Schiffer Publishing, Ltd.
4880 Lower Valley Road
Atglen, PA 19310
Phone: (610) 593-1777; Fax: (610) 593-2002
Email: Info@schifferbooks.com
Web: www.schifferbooks.com

For our complete selection of fine books on this and related subjects, please visit our website at www.schifferbooks.com. You may also write for a free catalog.

Schiffer Publishing's titles are available at special discounts for bulk purchases for sales promotions or premiums. Special editions, including personalized covers, corporate imprints, and excerpts, can be created in large quantities for special needs. For more information, contact the publisher.

We are always looking for people to write books on new and related subjects. If you have an idea for a book, please contact us at proposals@schifferbooks.com.

Acknowledgments

The author wishes to acknowledge the following for contributing photos to this project: John Gourley, USAF photo website, and the National Archives. In addition, the author wishes to thank Audrey Cohen and the staff of Epoch 5 Public Relations; Shelley LaRose-Arken, Mike Stack and the staff at Long Island MacArthur Airport for providing access to F-22 aircraft during landing events for the Jones Beach Airshow.

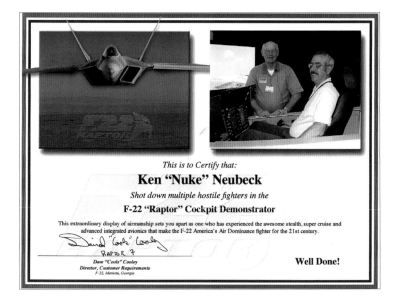

Author Ken Neubeck worked for a defense subcontractor that supplied equipment for the F-22, and he was the beneficiary of a "ride" in the F-22 Raptor cockpit demonstrator during a plant visit in 2008.

Contents

CHAPTER 1

F-22 Raptor Development

The YF-22 design by Lockheed would officially be designated as the F-22A Raptor in 1991. This F-22 Raptor is preparing for takeoff from Long Island MacArthur Airport during the F-22 demonstration team's participation in the 2022 Jones Beach Air Show. *Ken Neubeck*

The Lockheed Martin F-22A Raptor is a single-seat, twin-engine, all-weather stealth fighter that was developed for the US Air Force for the air-to-air-superiority fighter. It is considered a fifth-generation aircraft that was originally intended to be a replacement for the F-15 Eagle, a fourth-generation fighter that had no stealth capabilities when it was originally developed.

In 1981, a requirement for an advanced tactical fighter (ATF) was identified by the US Air Force, with this aircraft to replace the F-15 and F-16 aircraft that were currently in US Air Force service. This fighter was to take advantage of new technologies in fighter design that would make it lighter and stealthier.

Requirements for this aircraft were developed by the USAF beginning in 1983, and a formal request for proposal (RFP) was issued in 1985. Seven companies submitted bids, with two teams selected (Lockheed-Boeing and Northrop–McDonnell Douglas) to develop prototype aircraft for the demonstration/validation phase. At the same time, two engine designs were under consideration: the YF119 by Pratt & Whitney and the YF120 by General Electric. The Lockheed aircraft was designated the YF-22, and the Northrop–McDonnell Douglas aircraft would be designated the YF-23. Each team fielded two prototypes, with each prototype having different engines, with testing beginning in the fall of 1990.

In April 1991, Lockheed was announced as the winner, along with the F119 Pratt & Whitney engine being declared the winner for the engine design. While the YF-23 design had more stealth and was faster, the YF-22 was determined to be more maneuverable with the thrust-vectoring nozzles on the rear of the aircraft. It was deemed at the time that the YF-22 design was less expensive and risky.

The original planned quantity for this program was 750 aircraft, which was originally the expected need in 1985. However, this quantity would be reduced several times in the upcoming years as the original requirement was revised. In 1990, a review by Secretary of Defense Dick Cheney reduced the original quantity to 648 aircraft. However, there were further funding issues over the next few years, and this would cut this quantity significantly down to 339 aircraft in 1997. By 2003, this quantity was further reduced to 183 aircraft; however, in 2008, Congress would specify the final number to be 187 aircraft.

The reason for the reductions was due to cost and also the lack of US military action that required air-to-air missions during the wars that were fought at the time in Afghanistan (2001) and Iraq (2003). The F-22 would make occasional appearances in these wars, but in different roles than the original air-to-air-superiority role. Because of its stealth technology and classified features, the F-22 is banned from foreign export.

There was another study that was conducted with regard to reopening the production line for the F-22 in 2016 and possibly ordering an additional 194 aircraft. However, the costs in doing this action were prohibitive, with an estimated flyaway cost exceeding $200 million per aircraft, compared to the cost of $137 million for the last F-22 that rolled off the production line in 2011.

Prior to the development of the F-22 advanced tactical fighter (ATF), the F-15 Eagle was the USAF air-superiority fighter. The F-15 was considered a fourth-generation fighter, but it had no stealth capabilities designed into the airframe when it was developed. This F-15 is an outdoor display at the Wings of Eagle Museum in upstate New York. *Ken Neubeck*

The F-22 has been in service for over twenty-five years for the US Air Force. It has accrued, on average, 28,000 flight hours annually for the past dozen years. There have been five F-22 aircraft lost during its service time. *Ken Neubeck*

The first YF-22 ATF prototype aircraft (serial number [s/n] 87-0700) was presented during a formal ceremony held at Edwards AFB in front of USAF and company officials in August 1990. *USAF*

The first YF-22 ATF prototype aircraft (s/n 87-0700) would make its first flight in September 1990 at Edwards AFB. The aircraft is seen here in vertical flight during testing over the desert. *USAF*

The two YF-22 ATF prototypes are shown here at Edwards AFB in California during flight testing in 1990. YF-22 (s/n 87-0700) was equipped with the GE YF120 engine, and YF-22 (s/n 87-0701) was equipped with the P&W YF119 engine. After the F-22 won the competition, the P&W engine was chosen for the production version. *USAF*

YF-22 ATF prototype is flying over the desert at Edwards AFB in California. The first prototype made its first flight in September 1990, and the second YF-22 prototype made its first flight in October 1990. *USAF*

This is a desk model of the YF-23 ATF design by Northrop–McDonnell Douglas that competed in the flyoff against the YF-22 design by Lockheed Martin. The aircraft were not terribly different in appearance, with the most noticeable difference being the shape of the wings: the YF-22 wings were pitched back farther that the YF-23. *Ken Neubeck*

This is the YF-23 ATF or Black Widow II prototype aircraft (s/n 87-0800) as it rolls out at Edwards AFB, in June 1990. *USAF*

This is the first YF-23 Black Widow II prototype ATF aircraft (s/n 87-0800) during flight over the California desert, in September 1990. *USAF*

These are the YF-23 and the YF-22 ATF prototypes flying together over the desert during flight comparison in 1990. During the competition, the YF-23 was found to be stealthier and faster than the YF-22, but it was not as agile, and thus the F-22 design by Lockheed Martin was chosen to go into production. *USAF*

This is the first YF-22 Raptor prototype (s/n 87-0700), in fictitious marking as s/n 86-022, with tail code WA to be part of a static display model at Nellis AFB in preparation of the fiftieth anniversary of the US Air Force in April 1997. *USAF photo by SRA Brett K. Snow*

This is a front view of the first YF-22 Raptor prototype while on display at Nellis AFB. The two YF-22 prototypes flew seventy-four flights, with 91.6 flying hours accumulated during the flight-testing program, which was conducted at Edwards AFB, California. *USAF photo by SRA Brett K. Snow*

The first production F-22 was delivered in 1997. Originally, a quantity of 750 F-22s were projected to be purchased, but high program costs, production delays, an export band, and the lack of any adversary aircraft built by the Russians and Chinese resulted in several program cuts over the years, resulting in a final number of 195 production and EMD aircraft. *Ken Neubeck*

F-22 Raptor Specifications	
Length	62 feet, 1 inch
Height	16 feet, 8 inches
Wingspan	44 feet, 6 inches
Max. speed	Mach 2.2 (1,500 mph)
Max. to weight	83,500 pounds
Power plant	2 F119-PW-100 turbofans
Service ceiling	65,000 feet
Maximum range	1,800 miles (with two external fuel tanks)

CHAPTER 2

F-22 Raptor Program Summary

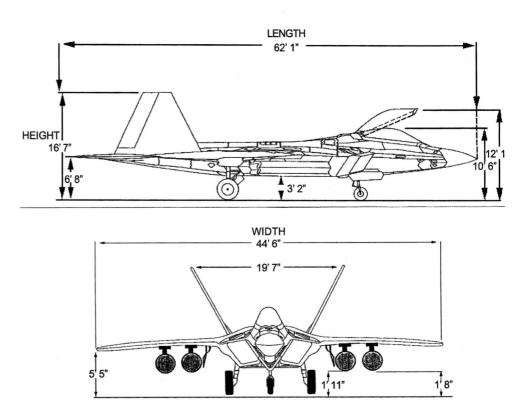

The first production model F-22 made its first flight on September 7, 1997. Originally, a quantity of 750 F-22s were planned to be purchased, but high program costs, production delays, an export ban, and the lack of any adversary aircraft built by the Russians and Chinese resulted in several cuts over the years, resulting in a final number of 187 production aircraft.

Early in the program, the F-22 was designated as the F/A-22 to simulate the Navy's F/A-18 designation for fighter/attack aircraft. This would change in 2005 by the US Air Force, with the official designation becoming the F-22A.

Type	Quantity	Tail Number
YF-22A Prototype	2	87-0700, 87-0701
F-22 EMD	9	91-4001–91-4009
F-22 PRTV*	2	99-4010–99-4011
F-22 Production (IP)	6	00-4012–00-4017
F-22 Production (LRIP** 1)	10	01-4018–01-4027
F-22 Production (LRIP 2)	13	02-4028–02-4040
F-22 Production (LRIP 3)	21	03-4041–03-4061
F-22 Production (Lot 4)	22	04-4062–04-4083
F-22 Production (Lot 5)	24	05-4084–05-4107
F-22 Production (Lot 6)	23	06-4108–06-4130
F-22 Production (Lot 7)	21	07-4131–07-4151
F-22 Production (Lot 8)	20	08-4152–08-4171
F-22 Production (Lot 9)	20	09-4172–09-4191
F-22 Production (Lot 10)	4	10-4192–10-4195
TOTALS	**195 F-22 and 2 YF-22 prototypes**	

* PRTV: production representative test vehicle

** LRIP: low-rate initial production

This is the F-22 Raptor final-production line in the Lockheed Martin plant located in Marietta, Georgia. The production line started in this plant in 1995 with preproduction F-22 aircraft and would end in December 2011, with the rollout of F-22 tail number 10-4195. *Lockheed Martin*

The last production F-22 Raptor (s/n 10-4195) is towed from the final-assembly area of Lockheed Martin on December 13, 2011, in Marietta, Georgia. *USAF photo by SA Danielle Purnell*

The last production F-22 Raptor is part of ceremonies at the Lockheed Martin Georgia plant in December 2011. In May, this aircraft would be assigned to the 525th FS, located in Joint Base at Elmendorf-Richardson. This aircraft has the initial tail code marking of AK. *USAF photo by SA Danielle Purnell*

The US Air Force F-22 Raptor is the United States' fifth-generation fighter, and with regard to stealth aircraft technology, it is considered fourth generation. It is banned from export to any foreign country, as upheld by the US Congress in 2006. *Ken Neubeck*

The US Air Force F-22 Raptor is the most expensive fighter aircraft to serve in the US Air Force. Cost estimates vary in terms of specific year dollar value, but one estimate regarding buying additional aircraft in 2017 was in the range of $200 million per aircraft. *Ken Neubeck*

In these photos, an F-22 Raptor is seen taking off from Long Island MacArthur Airport in New York after performing in the annual Jones Beach Air Show, in May 2022. This F-22 Raptor is one of two F-22 aircraft from Langley-Eustis AFB that performed demonstrations at air shows throughout the US in 2022. *Ken Neubeck*

Some F-22 crashes occurred during early field deployment. On November 15, 2012, an F-22 with tail number 00-4013 crashed at Tyndall AFB, Florida. The cause was due to a chaffed wire that arced and burned through an adjacent hydraulic line. The pilot ejected safely, but the aircraft was a complete loss. *USAF photo by Lisa Norman*

This particular F-22 Raptor was severely damaged during a belly landing in Nevada in April 2018. Due to extensive efforts by the personnel at the Joint Base Elmendorf Richardson, this aircraft was on the road to being full restored. This photo was taken in December 2021, and the aircraft was expected to fly again by mid-2022. *USAF photo A1C Michael Southerland*

CHAPTER 3
F-22 Raptor Details and Features

A pair of F-22 Raptors are parked on the tarmac at Long Island MacArthur Airport in May 2022. *Ken Neubeck*

The F-22 has design features that add to its stealth capability, which makes it a fourth-generation stealth aircraft as detailed in this chapter, along with several features that make it the fifth-generation air-superiority fighter. These features include the use of certain material in the aircraft structure and skin, along with the specific contour and shapes used throughout the aircraft.

There are no extrusions such as antennas sticking out from the various surfaces of the F-22. Rather, the various antennas are blended into the surfaces to help reduce the radar cross section (RCS) for the aircraft.

With the F-22, new technology brings new challenges, and these were addressed during the F-22 program. These new challenges include the maintenance of special coatings on the external surfaces, as well as various advances in software and electronic technology.

Indeed, after regular usage of the aircraft, with the stresses incurred from landings and takeoffs, there is some deterioration of the low observable (LO) coating on the surfaces of the airframe. Maintenance personnel inspect the coating regularly, inputting data measurements of the coating quality into an analytical program in a computer that rates the F-22's overall LO. If the number falls out of range, repair action is initiated on the surface coatings.

About 25 percent of the basic airframe is composite materials, which is used in the skin, wings, and tail (indicated as yellow in the diagram above). About 41 percent of the airframe weight is from titanium (shown as green in the diagram), which is used to reduce aircraft weight through its higher strength for its size.

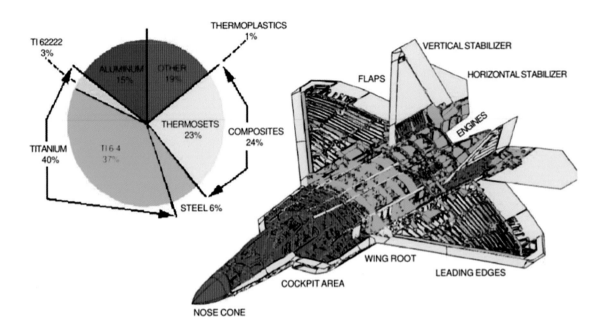

The stealth coatings on the skin surfaces of the F-22 are designed to be more robust and weather resistant than those used in earlier stealth aircraft. The stealth system accounts for almost one-third of maintenance, with the regular maintaining of all surface coatings being particularly demanding. *Ken Neubeck*

The F-22 has coatings on all surfaces that contribute to its stealth characteristics. Here a coating specialist applies the low-observable coating to a bare spot near the tail in a hangar located at Tyndall AFB, Florida. *USAF photo by A1C Alex Echols*

Compared to the B-2 and other USAF stealth aircraft, the F-22 surface coatings can be repaired in a regular hangar, in contrast to the need for special hangars for maintaining other stealth aircraft, thus saving money. The B-2 Spirit aircraft for example, requires complete restriping of the old coating and then applying new coating every seven years at a cost of $60. The F-22 has a less expensive process. *USAF photo by A1C Alex Echols*

Powered by two Pratt & Whitney F119-PW-100 turbofan engines, the US Air Force F-22 Raptor is the fastest fighter jet in the inventory, reaching speeds of Mach 2.25 (1,500 mph). The engines are very loud, with 146 decibels being recorded during testing when the afterburner is on, as seen in this photo. *USAF photo by 2Lt. Samuel Eckholm*

Seen here is the Pratt & Whitney F119 engine used on the F-22 undergoing operational testing and evaluation in May 2002. The engine is capable of providing 35,000 pounds of thrust. *USAF photo by SRA James T. May III*

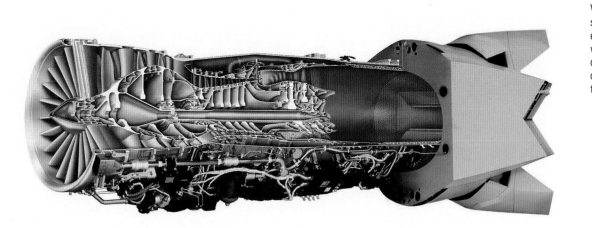

This cutaway view of the Pratt & Whitney F119 turbofan engine shows the different sections of the engine, beginning (*from the left*) with the fan section, the compressor section, and the combustor section, followed by the turbine section. *Pratt & Whitney*

Air National Guard personnel from the 192nd Maintenance Squadron, is performing pretest inspection on P&W F119 engine at Langley AFB in July 2015. *USAF photo by A1C Derek Seifert*

The F-22 Raptor has some advantages over existing USAF fighter aircraft, in that it can provide significantly more sorties each day than current fighters such as the F-15C. The F-22 can be flown on twice as many consecutive sorties, as well as being twice as reliable. With regard to maintenance, the F-22 requires one-half of the direct-maintenance man-hours per flight hour, as well as only two-thirds the turnaround time as the F-15C aircraft for its next combat sortie. *Ken Neubeck*

With regard to stealth features, the F-22 Raptor is less reliant on radar-absorbent material (RAM) compared to previous stealth aircraft design such as the F-117. Several features have been implemented into the F-22 airframe to reduce radar cross section (RCS), to aid in the aircraft being difficult to track by radar. This includes smooth surfaces and angled tail stabilizers. *Ken Neubeck*

The F-22 Raptor uses a gray camouflage paint scheme for all production aircraft. The F-22 Raptor pictured here has an overall gray on the fuselage, with darker-gray areas on portions of the wings, body, and tail, as seen here. *Ken Neubeck*

The F-22 Raptor gray paint scheme allows the aircraft to blend into the sky in many instances, with the darker areas of the paint scheme providing visual challenges to the naked human eye. *Ken Neubeck*

The F-22 Raptor consists of a nose landing gear and two main landing gears. This particular F-22 aircraft is situated on the tarmac at Long Island MacArthur Airport during participation at the 2009 Jones Beach Air Show. *Ken Neubeck*

This head-on view shows the landing-gear setup as well as the rectangular shape of the engine inlets of the F-22, along with the angled tail stabilizers. *USAF photo by SSgt. Peter Thompson*

This three-quarter view of an F-22 Raptor gives the perspective of the nose landing-gear location with respect to the main landing gears of the F-22. Also in this photo, the left-side weapons bay doors are open, with no missile loaded on the launcher. *Ken Neubeck*

This forward view of the F-22 Raptor during landing shows the location of the nose landing gear with respect to the main landing gears of the aircraft. In this view, the flaps are deployed. *Ken Neubeck*

Forward view of the F-22 shows the arrangement of the main landing gears and nose landing gear. There are two lights mounted on the nose landing-gear strut: a landing light and a taxi light. There are two rectangular engine inlets on each side of the fuselage. *Ken Neubeck*

A close-up view of the side and the front of the nose landing gear shows that the nosewheel is held by a fork structure. The nose landing gear uses a direct drive hydraulic system to turn the wheel. When the aircraft takes off, the landing gear pulls forward and the left and right doors of the nosewheel well close. *Ken Neubeck*

This is the left main landing gear for the F-22. During flight the gear pulls up in the wheel well area in the fuselage. The left-side weapons bay is located just in front of the landing gear. In this photo the left-side weapons bay is open, and it consists of two door panels mounted to the lower fuselage. The landing gear has its own bay inside the fuselage. *USAF photo by R. Nial Bradshaw*

A closer view of the left main landing gear shows that the strut rotates on a bar inside the fuselage and that there are several linkages attached. *USAF photo by TSgt. Jason Robertson*

Side view of the left main landing gear shows more details of the main landing-gear linkage. The three F-22 landing gear tires are steel-belted radial tires. *Ken Neubeck*

This view of an inverted F-22 Raptor during an air show performance shows how flush the underside of the aircraft is, when all landing gears are retracted. *John Gourley*

This top view of the F-22 Raptor during takeoff at Travis AFB, in 2019, shows the two different tones of gray used on the top of the aircraft. For this particular F-22 Raptor, darker gray is used on the nose section and on the leading and trailing edges of the wing and tail. *USAF photo by Heide Couch*

The glass canopy of the F-22 has a thin layer of indium tin oxide, which reflects radar waves as well as giving the glass a golden tint in appearance. The external boarding ladder used for the F-22 is located on the tarmac in this photo. *Ken Neubeck*

The pilot is using the external boarding ladder to exit the F-22 Raptor in Germany during its first European training deployment in August 2015. This particular aircraft features a different two-tone gray paint scheme, with the lighter gray used on the nose and the engine inlets. *USAF photo A1C Luke Kitterman*

The F-22 is a single-pilot cockpit that consists of a one-piece glass canopy that surrounds the pilot, which provides maximum visibility during flight. In this photo, the top of the console and the ejection seat can be seen. Note that there are two green emergency oxygen tanks located behind the ejection seat. *Ken Neubeck*

An F-22 Raptor canopy is seen here in the fully open position. The HUD glass display is on top of the front console, which extends from the forward part of the cockpit. *Ken Neubeck*

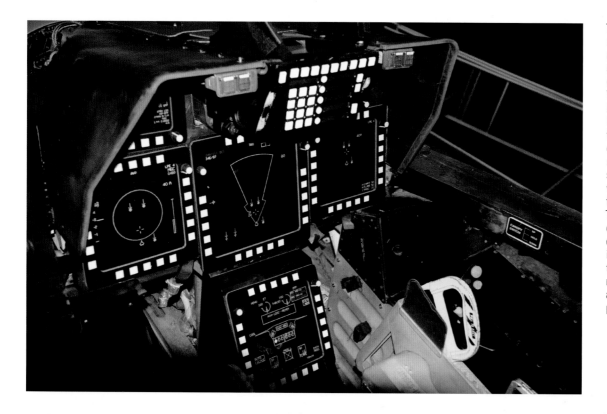

This main console is from the restored F-22 EMD (Engineering and Manufacturing Development) aircraft (s/n 91-4003) on static display at the USAF Museum at Wright-Patterson AFB, Dayton, Ohio. The aircraft is one of nine F-22 EMD aircraft, and it made its first flight in March 2000. The main console consists of four multifunction LCD displays that are set up on this restored aircraft, with simulated screens set up for flight control and weapon status. The heads-up display (HUD) control panel is located at the top of the console. Mission information that is displayed on the displays in an operational F-22 raptor cockpit would be classified and thus is not available to the public. *USAF*

An F-15 pilot from the 199th FS is in the F-22 cockpit simulator equipped with multifunction displays, which is laid out in similar fashion of an actual F-22 aircraft. The pilot is receiving instructions from a Lockheed Martin company trainer during training conducted at Hickam AFB, Hawaii. *USAF photo by MSgt. Kristen Stanley*

Perhaps the most captivating feature in the F-22 Raptor cockpit is the green illuminated heads-up display (HUD), located at the top of the instrument console, which can be seen from the front of the aircraft. Currently, F-22 pilots wear conventional helmets, without enhancements such as helmet-mounted displays, because of canopy space restrictions. Located in the front of the canopy are two white tubes that contain cartridge actuating devices (CAD) that are used to jettison the canopy during an emergency. *USAF photo by David Bedard*

This is a side view of the forward console, along with the HUD. F-22 pilot Maj. Paul Lopez is part of the F-22 Raptor demonstration team and is preparing for his certification flight while talking with his crew chief at Shaw AFB, South Carolina, in December 2017. *USAF photo by SSgt Zade Vadnais*

In this photo taken of an F-22 Raptor during aerial refueling from a KC-135 tanker, the reflection of the tanker aircraft can be seen on the HUD in the F-22. In addition, the pilot is fully geared up in his flight suit and oxygen mask, which would be the source of a USAF investigation in 2010 into a number of pilot hypoxia events during high-altitude flight. *USAF photo by A1C Kenneth W. Norman*

Lt. Col. Jay Flottmann, USAF flight surgeon and chief flight safety officer, speaks at a press conference in Washington, DC, on July 31, 2012, about the pilot hypoxia issue. He is demonstrating how a valve in the upper pressure garment and the shape and the size of the oxygen hoses on connections contributed to the physiological issues during F-22 flights at high altitude. *USAF photo by SA Christina Brownlow*

During the 2012 press conference held in Washington, DC, Maj. Gen. Charles Lyon shows a new valve design that will regulate the proper flow of oxygen to the F-22 pilot's vest. The valve went through qualification testing and was implemented into the fleet by the end of 2012. *USAF photo by SA Christina Brownlow*

In addition to the replacement of the faulty valve in the pilot's high-pressure vest, a filter in the oxygen system was removed in order to allow for a better flow in the system. The pilot in this photo is wearing the improved vest. *USAF photo by MSgt. Russ Scalf*

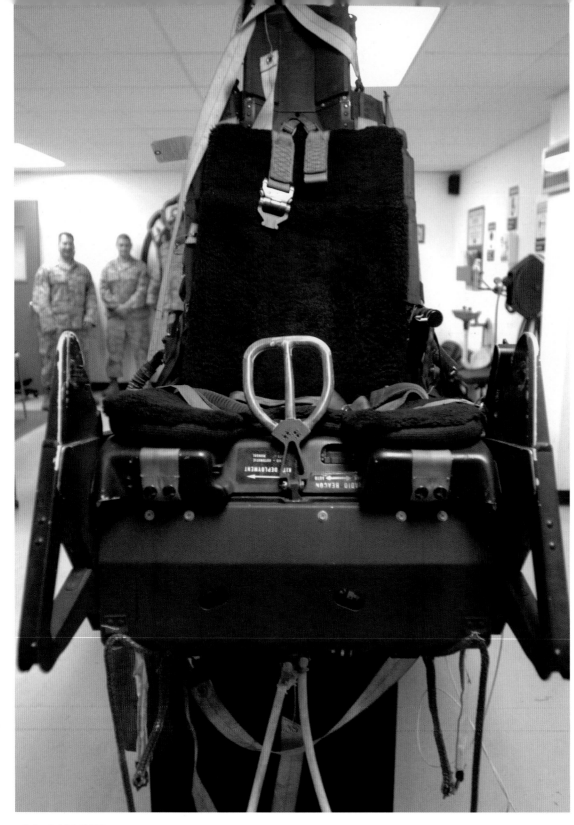

The F-22 Raptor uses an Advanced Concept Ejection Seat II (ACES II). This is an ACES II seat that has not been installed into the F-22, and it has gone through a preflight inspection at the maintenance egress shop. The ACES II is used on other USAF aircraft, with some differences. For the F-15, there are gas lines located in the seat, whereas the F-22 has electrical circuitry that is used to trigger a series of synapses to orchestrate the ejection process. A telescoping rocket is affixed to the back of the seat, which propels the seat from the cockpit. The ejection handle is located in the front of the seat, between the pilot's legs. *USAF photo by A1C Jason J. Brown*

ACES II Ejection Seat diagram above shows the location of major components in the ejection seat system.

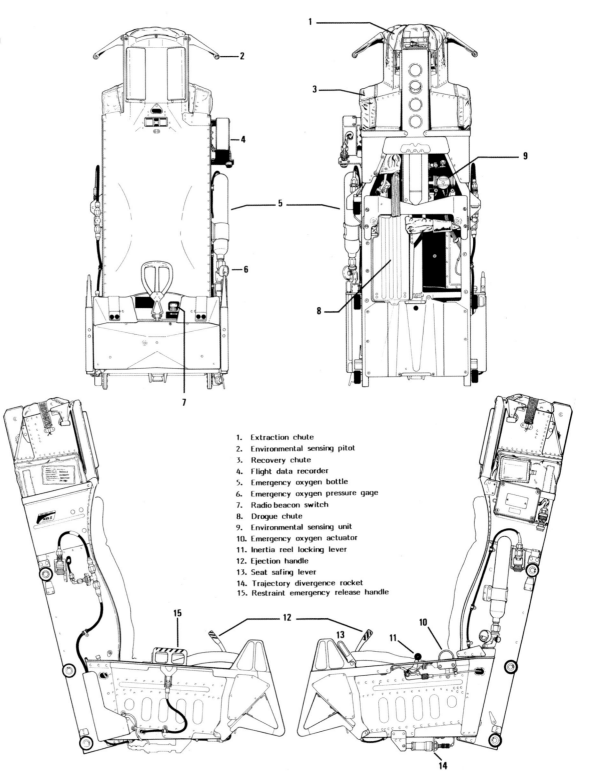

1. Extraction chute
2. Environmental sensing pitot
3. Recovery chute
4. Flight data recorder
5. Emergency oxygen bottle
6. Emergency oxygen pressure gage
7. Radio beacon switch
8. Drogue chute
9. Environmental sensing unit
10. Emergency oxygen actuator
11. Inertia reel locking lever
12. Ejection handle
13. Seat safing lever
14. Trajectory divergence rocket
15. Restraint emergency release handle

F-22 Raptor is preparing for takeoff from Joint Base Langley-Eustis, Virginia, with HUD in the cockpit noticeable. *USAF photo by 2Lt. Sam Eckholm*

In contrast to the F-15 Eagle tail section, where there is a straight vertical stabilizer section, the F-22 Raptor has angled tail stabilizers in the tail section. The angle is 55 degrees from the horizontal plane and is part of the stealth aspect of the design to reduce RCS or radar signature. *Ken Neubeck*

The rear of the F-22 Raptor has several distinct features. The structure at the rear of the wing is the flaperon, in front of the composite tailplane structure. There is a rudder section that is located at the rear of each stabilizer section of the tail. Near the leading edge of each stabilizer section is the formation lighting strip. *Ken Neubeck*

The F-22 Raptor has a very distinctive protruding rear section of the aircraft that contains the two titanium engine exhaust sections that are vector controlled for directing the thrust from the exhaust. *John Gourley*

This view of the rear of the Raptor shows the two rectangular shape exhaust sections, along with weapons crew loading bombs into the center weapons bay. The exhaust section are covered by protective covers when on the ground and removed before flight, and the lanyard located between the exhaust section is for the pin on the emergency arresting hook, which is also removed before flight. *USAF photo by SSgt. Sandra Welch*

When on the ground, the lower thrust-vectoring panels are covered to protect the panels from damage during ground maintenance, as well as protecting the ground crew from injury. *Ken Neubeck*

This view of an F-22 Raptor in a steep climb shows the afterburner flame from the vector-controlled twin exhaust section. Each exhaust section contains an upper and lower panel structure. It is also noted that there is water vapor coming off the top part of the aircraft during this climb. *John Gourley*

In this view of the right top side of the F-22, it can be seen that there are several panels and antennas that are blended with the skin of the aircraft, to aid in the stealth features of the F-22 by avoiding extruded antennas. The dark-gray jagged-shape panel in the middle is the right-side air-cooled fuel cooler (ACFC) duct, which helps cool the hot fuel. Antennas such as the wing root EW antenna and the communications/navigation/identification (CNI) band antennas are part of the right leading-edge flap. Located on the left side of this photo is the flip-up door for the cannon muzzle. *Ken Neubeck*

Several details of the F-22 Raptor can be seen in this top view of the aircraft. The open doors located on top of the fuselage, behind the cockpit, are for the aerial-refueling receptacle. There are antennas that located on the leading edge of each wing, including the CNI Band 2 forward antennas and the ILS localizer antennas. *USAF photo by SA Brittany A. Chase*

In this photo, an aerial-refueling boom from a KC-135 tanker is engaging with the refueling receptable inside the opened refueling door on the F-22. *USAF photo by TSgt. Abigail Klein*

Ground crew is performing a "hot pit" refuel on an F-22 Raptor during operations conducted in May 2013 at Joint Base Elmendorf-Richards, Alaska. Entry for refueling is through the ground refuel receptable that is located on the left side of the aircraft. *USAF photos by TSgt. Dana Ross*

In this sequence of photos, maintainers are preparing to refuel an F-22 Raptor at Joint Base Elmendorf in August 2021, using the port located on the top of the aircraft that is usually used for aerial refueling. This type of refueling is done during certain operational exercises. *USAF photos by SA Marcus M. Bullock*

A KC-135 Stratotanker is refueling three F-15 Strike Eagles and one F-22 Raptor aircraft during refueling training exercises in January 2009. *USAF photo by MSgt. Scott Reed*

A pair of F-22 Raptors are preparing for refueling from an Air National Guard (ANG) KC-135 over Alaska in March 2008. *USAF photo by A1C Jonathan Steffen*

The F-22 has two side internal weapons bays and a main internal weapons bay, which are closed until the point of weapon release. The F-22 also has hardpoints under each wing for carrying external weapons or external fuel tanks. *Ken Neubeck*

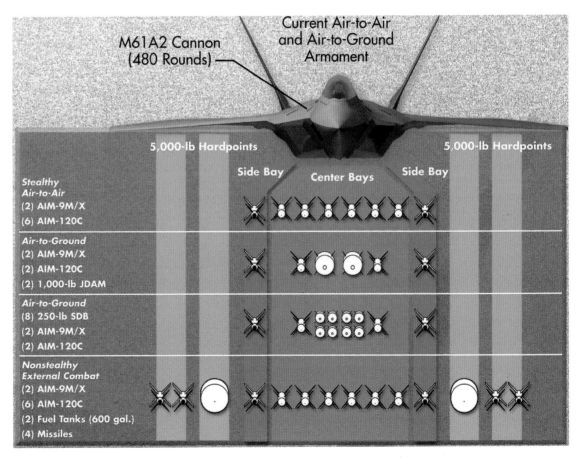

M61A2 Cannon (480 Rounds)

Current Air-to-Air and Air-to-Ground Armament

5,000-lb Hardpoints   5,000-lb Hardpoints

Side Bay   Center Bays   Side Bay

Stealthy Air-to-Air
(2) AIM-9M/X
(6) AIM-120C

Air-to-Ground
(2) AIM-9M/X
(2) AIM-120C
(2) 1,000-lb JDAM

Air-to-Ground
(8) 250-lb SDB
(2) AIM-9M/X
(2) AIM-120C

Nonstealthy External Combat
(2) AIM-9M/X
(6) AIM-120C
(2) Fuel Tanks (600 gal.)
(4) Missiles

This diagram above shows the different weapon configurations for the different missions that the F-22 Raptor flies. *Lockheed Martin*

To aid in the stealth aspects of the F-22 Raptor, the four weapons bay doors (two side bays, and left and right main bays) remain closed until the time that the weapons are ready to be released. *Jim Petty*

In this photo, it can be seen that the F-22 Raptor has two distinct side-by-side left and right main weapons bays that are located in the lower fuselage, as seen on this F-22 with the weapons bay doors open. Each weapons bay contains three AMRAAM vertical eject launchers (AVELs) that are attached to the ceiling and extend about 2 feet downward in order for the missiles to clear the aircraft. *Jim Petty*

A weapons loader is preparing to load an AIM 120 missile to one of the AVELs that are located in the left main weapons bay of the F-22, during load crew competition held at Joint Base Elmendorf-Richardson, Alaska, in April 2012. *USAF photo by TSgt. Dana Rosso*

This is a close-up view of the LAU-142/A AMRAAM vertical eject launcher in the extended position while undergoing functional testing. The AVEL is a combination pneumatic/hydraulic device that carries AIM-120C missiles in the F-22 Raptor's center weapons bays and extends during firing for safe aircraft separation as high speeds. *Ken Neubeck*

This photo shows the right and left portions of the main weapons bay. One portion has the three AVELs in retracted position, and in the other portion there is one AVEL on the ceiling while a weapons loader is installing a BRU-47 bomb rack on the inboard side, near the center beam. The bomb rack will be used to carry a GBU-32 Joint Direct Attack Munition (JDAM). *USAF photo by Samuel King Jr.*

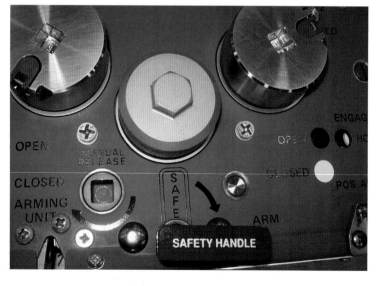

The operational side of the bomb rack shows two cylinders for holding explosive cartridges to open hooks during release in flight, along with a square drive for ground crew to manually open the hooks when loading stores. *Ken Neubeck*

A weapons loader is using a socket wrench with a square drive on the BRU-47 bomb rack to manually open the hooks, in preparation for loading the GBU-32 JDAM. *USAF photo by 2Lt. Karissa Rodriguez*

An airman checks the GBU-32 JDAM after it was loaded just prior into the right portion of the main weapons bay of the F-22 Raptor during a load crew competition that was held at Joint Base Elmendorf-Richardson, Alaska, in July 2017. The JDAM has an attachment kit mounted to the middle of the store, and contains a guidance system that allows the pilot to guide it to the target. *USAF photo by SA Johnathan Steffen*

Weapons loader personnel are using a cart to bring a GBU-32 JDAM for loading into the F-22 aircraft. The GBU-32 weighs 1,013 pounds and requires a weapons loader vehicle to bring the JDAM up to the bomb rack in the main weapons bay. *USAF photo by 2Lt. Karissa Rodriguez*

In this photo, the GBU-32 JSAM has been removed from the cart and is on a BL-1 weapons loader vehicle to aid in loading into the F-22 aircraft. The gray brackets installed on the GBU-32 are body strakes, which add stability and lift to the JDAM. *USAF photo by TSgt. Michael R. Holzworth*

In this photo, the left-side weapons bay door is open, and the left-side door of the main weapons bay door is open. *Ken Neubeck*

The right-side weapons bay is identical to the left-side weapons bay. Pictured here is the weapons rail that will extend out from the bay when the doors open during the firing of air-to-air missiles such as the AIM-9 Sidewinder. *Ken Neubeck*

A weapons loader secures an inert AIM-9 Sidewinder missile to the left-side weapons bay of an F-22 Raptor during a load crew competition on Joint Base Elmendorf-Richardson, Alaska, in July 2015. Load crew competitions are held regularly to sharpen weapons loader's skills. *USAF photo by Alejandro Pena*

A weapons loader verifies that an inert AIM-9 Sidewinder missile is properly secured to the LAU-141/A Trapeze Launcher located in the left-side weapons bay. This launcher extends via hydraulic control. *USAF photo by R. Nial Bradshaw*

An F-22 Raptor launches an AIM-9 missile from the left-side weapons bay during testing in March 2005 at the USN Naval Air Warfare Center in China Lake, California. The AIM-9X missile has a range of up to 22 miles. *US Navy photo*

A pair of F-22 Raptors from the 94th FS release GBU-32 JDAMs (Joint Direct Attack Munition) during the ninety-fifth anniversary of Maj. Billy Mitchell bombing of the German warship *Ostfriesland*, that was used for post–World War I target practice off Cape Henry. The GBU-32 has a range of up to 15 miles. *US Navy photo*

The F-22 Raptor is equipped with an M61A1 cannon, manufactured by General Dynamics, and it is located on the right side of the aircraft, at midfuselage, as can be seen by the indentations on the top surface in this photo. The cannon is considered a secondary weapons system for the Raptor, because the AIM-9 missile is used more for the aerial combat role since they can be fired at greater distances at enemy aircraft. *USAF photo by TSgt. Ben Bloker*

When the cannon is fired, a door is open for the 20 mm shells to exit, as seen here during gun-firing tests held at Edwards AFB in 2002. *USAF photo by Judson Brohmer*

The M61 cannon is used on other US military aircraft such as the F-16 Falcon and the F/A-18 Super Hornet. It can fire 20 mm rounds at the rate of 6,000 rounds per minute, and the ammo drum used on the F-22 Raptor holds up to 480 rounds. *General Dynamics*

CHAPTER 4
F-22 Raptor Squadrons

Two F-22A Raptors from the F-22 demonstration team from Langley-Eustis AFB have arrived at Long Island MacArthur Airport for participation in the 2022 Jones Beach Air Show. *Ken Neubeck*

There have been eleven different USAF squadrons that had the F-22 aircraft in their service. At the current time, there are ten active squadrons based at four different locations throughout the United States, with three squadrons each operating out of Alaska and Florida and two squadrons each out of Virginia and Hawaii.

Of interest is that each base has unique F-22 missions. The F-22 squadrons based at Elmendorf AFB, Alaska, see their main mission as the regular intercept of Russian aircraft flying in the international airspace near the Arctic Circle. The F-22 aircraft based in Langley-Eustis AFB, Virginia, are used during the F-22 demonstration team that flies at air shows throughout the US on a yearly basis. The F-22s from Hickam AFB, Hawaii, provide US fighter aircraft presence in the Pacific Ocean.

A number of these F-22 Raptor squadrons have been deployed in different war theaters for combat activity in recent years. These are typically temporary deployments, and there has been no long-term assignment of the F-22 to any foreign base.

F-22 aircraft on a yearly basis will be used as part of the demonstration team that participates in various air shows conducted in the United States.

Squadron	Nickname	Location	Tail Code
7th FS*	Bunyips	Holloman AFB, NM	HO
19th FS	Fighting Gamecocks	Hickam AFB, HI	HH
27th FS	Fightin' Eagles	Langley-Eustis AFB, VA	FF
43rd FS	American Hornets	Tyndall AFB, FL	TY
90th FS	Pair of Dice	Elmendorf AFB, AK	EL
94th FS	Hat in the Ring Gang	Langley-Eustis AFB, VA	FF
95th FS	Boneheads	Tyndall AFB, FL	TY
199th FS	Mytai Fighters	Hickam AFB, HI	HH
301st FW (ARES)	Red Tail Angels	Tyndall AFB, FL	TY
302nd FS	Sun Devils	Elmendorf AFB, AK	EL
525th FS	Bulldogs	Elmendorf AFB, AK	EL

* squadron deactivated

A pair of F-22 Raptors from the 7th FS are flying over the White Sands Missile Range in New Mexico on the way to Holloman AFB, New Mexico, in June 2008. *USAF photo by SA Russel Scalf*

A 7th FS F-22 Raptor on the runway at Holloman AFB in June 2013. This squadron flew as part of Operation Noble Eagle (ONE) in support of homeland security operations after the 9/11 attacks. The squadron would be deactivated in 2014, with aircraft sent to Tyndall AFB during consolidation. *USAF photo by A1C Aaron Montoya*

A 7th FS F-22 Raptor taking off from the runway at Holloman AFB in February 2012. The tail code for this aircraft is HO. *USAF photo by A1C Daniel E. Liddecoet*

The F-22 would be active at Holloman AFB for only a six-year period, from 2008 through 2014. When the squadron was deactivated during base reductions in the US, the F-22 from that base was transferred to squadrons located at other US bases. *USAF photo by A1C Daniel E. Liddecoet*

A 19th FS F-22 Raptor on the runway at Hickam AFB, Hawaii. The 19th FS and the 199th FS ANG unit are essentially a combined squadron, sharing the available F-22 aircraft based at this location between the two squadrons. *USAF photo by SSgt. Nathan Allen*

F-22 Raptors from the 19th FS and the 199th FS, both based at Hickam AFB, Hawaii, are taxiing down the runway single file during joint participation in Operation Sentry in December 2018. *USAF photo by SA John Linzmeier*

These photos show F-22 Raptors from the 19th FS and the 199th FS, both based at Hickam AFB, Hawaii, being serviced in special structures known as "alert pads" that are located near the runway. This special setup allows for quicker turnaround time for the F-22 aircraft on the flight line.
USAF photo by SSgt. Nathan Allen

This F-22 Raptor (s/n 03-4042) is the first Raptor assigned to the 27th FS in Langley, in May 2005. *USAF photo by TSgt. Ben Bloker*

Lt. Col. James Hecker flies an F-22 Raptor over Fort Monroe prior delivery to the 27th Fighter Squadron in May 2005. This was the first F-22 Raptor that was delivered to this base. *USAF photo by TSgt. Ben Bloker*

A pair of F-22 Raptors from the 27th FS are on the tarmac at Long Island MacArthur Airport as their base for the May 2008 Jones Beach Air Show. *Ken Neubeck*

This F-22 Raptor from the 27th FS is seen flying out of Lakenheath AB, located in the UK, in October 2017. *USAF photo by SA Malcolm Mayfield*

F-22 Raptor (s/n 01-4018) is the first Raptor to be delivered to the 43rd FS, located at Tyndall AFB in the Panhandle area of Florida, in September 2003. *USAF photo by TSgt. Mike Ammons*

Waiting on the tarmac are maintenance crews and others as Maj. Max Moroska delivers this F-22 Raptor (s/n 02-4028), the seventh Raptor overall to be delivered to the 43rd FS in Tyndall AFB, in August 2004. *USAF photo by Steve Wallace*

An F-22 Raptor (s/n 01-4022) from the 43rd FS has the afterburners on during participation in Sentry Savannah operation in August 2016. *USAF photo by SA Solomon Cook*

An F-22 Raptor (s/n 03-4042) from the 43rd FS is shown leaving Wright-Patterson AFB, Ohio, to return to Florida in September 2020. Several F-22 Raptors from Tyndall were evacuated to Ohio due to tropical storms that were passing through Florida at this time. It is noted that this particular F-22 Raptor was originally assigned to the 27th FS in Langley (*see previous pages*). *USAF photo by A1C Alexandria Fulton*

This F-22 Raptor from the 90th FS (Pair-o-Dice) is participating in Red Flag exercises at Eielson AFB, Alaska, in August 2014. This squadron features the AK tail code. *USAF photo by SSgt. Jim Araos*

Seven F-22 Raptors from the 90th FS are on the field of Yokota AB, Japan, after having been relocated from Kadena AB because of Typhoon Maria in July 2018. The deployment of the squadron to Japan was part of Pacific theater security exercises. *USAF photo by Yasuo Osakabi*

An F-22 Raptor from the 90th FS is taking off from Elmendorf-Richardson Joint AFB, Alaska, during Red Flag exercises held in August 2015. *USAF photo by Alejandro Pena*

F-22 Raptors from the 90th FS are part of the F-22 demonstration team that is performing maneuvers during the Australian International Airshow and Aerospace Exposition (AVALON) in March 2017. *USAF photo by MSgt. John Gordinier*

The 94th FS (Hat in the Ring FS), located at Langley AFB, Virginia, received F-22 Raptors in 2006. Seen here is a four-ship formation of F-22 Raptors from the 94th DA flying in formation over the Rocky Mountain range in Colorado during the return trip back to Joint Base Langley-Eustis, Virginia, after participating in Operation Red Flag in August 2017. *USAF photo by SSgt. Carlin Leslie*

F-22 Raptor (s/n 04-067) from the 94th FS is on the tarmac at Long Island MacArthur Airport in New York, during its participation in the Jones Beach Air Show in May 2022. *Ken Neubeck*

F-22 Raptor (s/n 09-178) from the 94th FS is on deployment at Nellis AFB, Nevada, in August 2017, for participation in Red Flag exercises. The exercises are held yearly with other participating units to engage in simulated combat training for three weeks. *USAF photos by SSgt. Carlin Leslie*

Four F-22 Raptors are shown here undergoing preflight checks at Nellis AFB, Nevada, in August 2017, during the squadron's participation in Red Flag exercises. Target areas for the exercises are located north of the Air Force base. *USAF photos by SSgt. Carlin Leslie*

F-22 Raptors from the 95th FS are flying over the Baltic Sea as part of a four-aircraft deployment to Spandahlem AB, Germany, in September 2015. *USAF photo by TSgt. Jason Robertson*

Three F-22 Raptors from the 95th FS are participating in Red Flag exercises over Nellis AFB, Nevada, in July 2014. A total of twelve F-22s and 120 personnel made the trip for this exercise. *USAF photo by A1C Thomas Spangler*

Four F-22 Raptors from the 199th FS are participating in a dynamic force employment (DFE) event to Marine Corps Air Station, Iwakuni, Japan, in March 2021. DFE involves the rapid transition to combat operations. *USAF photo by LCpl. Triton Lai*

An F-22 Raptor (s/n 05-4098) of the 199th FS is being serviced by ground personnel during the DFE event. *USAF photo by LCpl. Triton Lai*

This Air Force reserve F-22 Raptor (s/n 05-098) is from the 301st FS, based at Tyndall, and is landing in Poland as part of training exercises in August 2015. *USAF photo by SSgt. Joe W. McFadden*

F-22 Raptor aircraft from the 301st FS are on deployment to Hill AFB during exercises Combat Hammer and Combat Archer in August 2016. The exercises focused on the loading of weapons by airmen and the pilot firing these weapons in flight. *USAF photo by R. Nial Bradshaw*

An F-22 Raptor (s/n 05-4102) from the 302nd FS (Sun Devils) is seen here at Elmendorf-Richardson Joint AFB, Anchorage, Alaska, in October 2012. The pilot has placed a folded US flag on top of the console in front of the HUD. *USAF Reserve photo by TSgt. Dana Rosso*

The 302nd FS was previously located at Luke AFB, Texas, and was relocated to Alaska in 2007, at which time the squadron converted to F-22 aircraft. The Alaska mountain range is located east of the AFB and is seen here in the background. *USAF Reserve photo by TSgt. Dana Rosso*

This F-22 from the 302nd FS is flying over Anchorage, Alaska, during a routine training mission in April 2008. *USAF photo by TSgt. Keith Brown*

A pair of F-22 Raptors from the 302nd FS are flying over the mountain range in Alaska in March 2015. *USAF photo by TSgt. Dana Rosso*

An F-22 Raptor from the 525th FS based at Elmendorf-Richardson AFB is shown taking off during Operation Red Flag in April 2009. The base is located north of Anchorage, Alaska, and west of mountain ranges in Chugach State Park, as seen in the background of this photo. *USAF photo by SA Laura Turner*

An F-22 Raptor is on the tarmac, awaiting refueling at Kadena AFB, located in Okinawa, Japan, during exercises held in March 2011. *USAF photo by A1C Maeson L. Elleman*

An F-22 Raptor assigned to the 525th Fighter Squadron from Joint Base Elmendorf-Richardson, Alaska, flies away after aerial refueling during Exercise Northern Edge, over Alaska. *USAF photo by SSgt. Micaiah Anthony*

An F-22 Raptor assigned to Joint Base Elmendorf-Richardson, Alaska, flies in formation over the Joint Pacific Alaska Range Complex in July 2019. This complex is over 67,000 square miles and provides the room for all types of training for the F-22 mission. *USAF photo by SSgt. James Richardson*

CHAPTER 5
F-22 Combat Activity

A lone F-22 Raptor takes off in the early dawn hours prior to taking part in a combat mission over Syria on September 23, 2014, in which a Syrian command center would be attacked. *USAF photo by TSgt. Russell Scalf*

The F-22 Raptor entered operational service in the US Air Force beginning in 2003, well after the initial phases of Operation Enduring Freedom in Afghanistan in 2001 and Operation Iraqi Freedom in 2003. Most F-22 squadrons would become operational units by 2009, during the later stages of these conflicts.

Indeed, the F-22 Raptor would make an appearance in the Middle East in November 2009 as part of Operation Iron Falcon. However, many of the deployments at this time by the F-22 in Iraq and Syria were kept vague with regard to specific missions and were referred generally to as deployments in Southwest Asia.

Against ISIS forces located in Iraq and Syria, the first major F-22 combat action took place in September 23, 2014, when four F-22 Raptors were part of a bombing raid on a command center located in Syria near the Turkish border. Over the next ten months, the F-22 Raptor would fly over two hundred sorties in sixty locations, dropping 270 bombs.

For many of the combat missions in this region, the Raptor would be used primarily as an escort and surveillance aircraft to team up in protecting other USAF strike aircraft during bombing raids such as by the F-16 and F-15. By its presence with these aircraft in Syria, where there are significant air defenses, the F-22 Raptor's primary role was to dominate the sky, so that it keeps other air forces down on the ground, thus protecting the other USAF airplanes that are not as good in the air-to-air role. Final defeat of ISIS in Syria took place in March 2019.

The F-22 would be used for the first time in Afghanistan on November 19, 2017, when it was used with other aircraft to destroy eight Taliban opium production facilities in Helmand Province. The F-22 was used because it had the capability to carry small-diameter precision bombs. F-22s took off from Al Dhafra Air Base in the UAE and underwent aerial refueling.

F-22 Raptors were deployed in the Middle East region, making appearances there as early as 2009. Shown here are F-22 Raptors from Langley AFB participating in Iron Falcon exercises at an undisclosed location in Southwest Asia in November 2009. *USAF photo by TSgt. Charles Larkin Sr.*

An F-22 Raptor from 1st FW from Joint Base Langley-Eustis is undergoing refueling from a KC-10 tanker after being deployed for a bombing mission over Syria, on September 23, 2014. *USAF photo by Maj. Jefferson S. Heiland*

These unclassified photos show the before-and-after results of a bombing attack on September 23, 2014, by four F-22 Raptor aircraft from the 1st FW from Joint Base Langley-Eustis on an ISIS command and control center. This command center was located in Raqquah, Syria, near the Euphrates River, not far from the Turkish border. The F-22 aircraft used laser-guided GBUs to inflict damage specifically to only the right side of the building, where the command and control center was located. *DoD photo*

Although the F-22 was not used significantly during early combat activity in the Middle East in Operation Iraqi Freedom, the aircraft would be used more in August 2015, when it was adapted for close-air-support (CAS) missions in Syria against ISIS as part of Operation Inherent Resolve, against artillery and command posts. An F-22 Raptor is seen in the distance at a forward base in the region. *USAF photo by SSgt. Sandra Welch*

Weapons loaders are preparing to load JDAM ordnance on F-22s at forward base in an undisclosed section of Iraq in August 2015, during action against ISIS forces in the region. *USAF photo by SSgt. Sandra Welch*

Opium is a major economic driver for the Taliban in Afghanistan, with massive opium fields located in Helmand Province. F-22 aircraft were used in conducting bombing raids in 2017 on opium production facilities that are used to process opium from fields in this province. *USMC photo by Cpl. John McCall*

A major reason for using the F-22 Raptor for raids on opium facilities in Afghanistan in 2017 was its ability to release the GBU-39 small-diameter bombs (SDB), which are high precision for specific targets and less likely to cause civilian casualties. The GBU-39 SDBs are seen here attached to their bomb rack unit, which will be mounted inside the F-22 Raptor's weapons bay. *USAF photo by TSgt. Dana Rosso*

A major reason for using the F-22 Raptor for raids on opium facilities in Afghanistan in 2017 was its ability to release the GBU-39 small-diameter bombs (SDB) that are high precision for specific targets and less likely to cause civilian casualties. The photos provided here show F-22 aircraft originally from Tyndall that are part of the 95th Expeditionary Fighter Squadron leaving Al Dhafra Airbase in the United Arab Emirates (UAE) for their mission to bomb drug facilities in Afghanistan, on November 19, 2017. *USAF photo by TSgt. Anthony Nelson*

An F-22 Raptor assigned to the 380th Air Expeditionary Wing is taking off from Al Dhafra AB, UAE, in a night mission for Operation Inherent Resolve support in February 2018. *USAF photo by TSgt Anthony Nelson Jr.*

Top-view photo of an F-22 Raptor is taken from the refueling tanker during an OIR mission in March 2018. The pilot and the predominant HUD can be seen. *USAF photo by TSgt. Anthony Nelson Jr.*

This F-22 Raptor from the 380th Air Expeditionary Force is preparing for takeoff during a mission in attacking ISIS ground in December 2016. *USAF photo by SA Tyler Woodward*

A pair of F-22 Raptors deployed from Langley AFB are in Syria conducting airstrikes on selected ISIS targets in November 2019. *USAF photo by MSgt. Joshua L. Demotts*

These photos show F-22 Raptors from the 95th Expeditionary Fighter Squadron, which was based at Al Dhafra Airbase. The aircraft have just finished refueling during their participation in Operation Inherent Resolve over Syria in March 2018. *USAF photos by SSgt Colton Elliot*

This series of photos shows the F-22 Raptor flying over the Iraq region, near the Euphrates River area sands, after refueling. The F-22 is part of a deployment to the Al Dhafra Air Base, in November 2019, as part of Operation Resolve. The F-22 has been flying over Syria for more than three years in roles as a fighter escort as well as a "quarterback" for directing fighter attack groups. *USAF photo by TSgt. Anthony Nelson Jr.*

CHAPTER 6
F-22 Raptor NORAD Intercept Role

An F-22 is in the foreground, with a Tupolev Tu-95 bomber in the background, during an intercept event in international air space near Alaska, on March 9, 2020. *NORAD*

The F-22 Raptor has been brought into the role of intercept role for shadowing Russian aircraft that fly in international airspace near US airspace in the northern part of Alaska, as well as in other areas in the Arctic zones. The F-22 aircraft are based at Elmendorf AFB, near Anchorage, and are assigned to North American Aerospace Defense Command (NORAD).

This cat-and-mouse game has been going on for years, with different US fighter aircraft that typically were based out of Alaska being involved. Typically, there may be one or two Russians Tupolev Tu-95 bombers that may or may not be accompanied by Sukhoi Su-35 fighters.

The F-22 Raptor has been involved in the interceptor role in this region of the world since 2015. Sometimes, there may be more than one such event occurring in a month, as was the case in September 2018.

The intercept role for US fighter aircraft had its origins more than fifty years ago, beginning during the Cold War era, when US fighters such as the F-102 and F-4 conducted such flights. These events are almost considered routine during the new millennium as well.

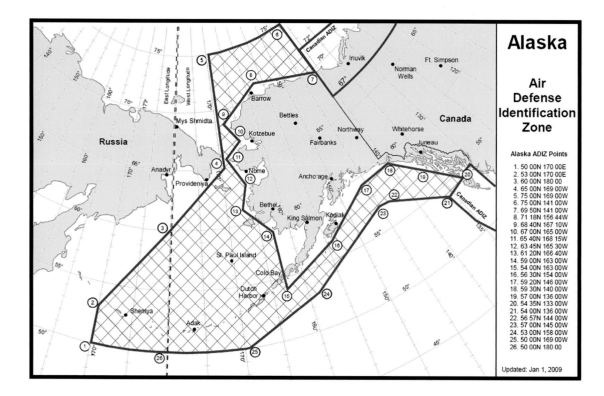

The area of coverage for the Air Defense Identification Zone (ADIZ) is shown on this map of the Alaska region of the US, in which twenty-six distinct zones are established. The F-22 Raptor is one of the principal aircraft that is involved in this role for NORAD as an interceptor. *FAA*

In this photo, an F-22 Raptor is performing the initial intercept, where it rides side by side with the Tu-95 intercontinental bomber during the identification phase in June 2020. Typically, no further action occurs beyond this "escort" role. *NORAD*

F-22 intercepts a Russian Tu-95 bomber off the coast of Alaska and California on May 22, 2019. The Tu-95 is nicknamed the "Bear" and has been in service since 1952. Approximately two dozen Tu-95 aircraft are still in service and are intercepted in the Arctic Circle. *NORAD*

An F-22 rides along the left side of a Russian Tu-95 bomber near Alaska on May 26, 2019. Top speed for the Tu-95 is 525 mph, well within the capability of the F-22 to intercept this aircraft and ride alongside it. *NORAD*

A pair of F-22 Raptors are flying over the mountain range near the Joint Base Elmendorf-Richardson in July 2019. This base is the northernmost US base and is key in the NORAD mission of tracking intruder aircraft to protected airspace in this region. *USAF photo by SSgt James Richardson*

An "elephant walk" is being conducted at Joint Base Elmendorf-Richardson in Alaska of all the USAF aircraft assigned there in 2020. Twenty-six F-22s lead the way in front of C-130, E-3, and C-17 aircraft. *NORAD*

These cat-and-mouse intercept events continue up to the current time. On October 19, 2020, F-22 Raptors from the Elmendorf-Richardson AFB were deployed to intercept two Russian Tu-95 bombers and two Su-35 fighters, as shown in these two photos. *NORAD*

CHAPTER 7

F-22 Raptor Demo Team Maneuvers

The F-22 Raptor demonstration team has its own dedicated emblem, which is located on the F-22 Demo Team's support truck that goes to the different air show locations to support the team's aircraft. *Ken Neubeck*

Like other USAF aircraft teams such as the Thunderbirds and F-16 demo team, the US Air Force has a dedicated F-22 demonstration team that performs various aerial maneuvers each year at air shows located throughout the US. These maneuvers demonstrate some of the awesome and unique capabilities of the F-22, the world's premier fifth-generation aircraft.

The F-22 Raptor demonstration team is stationed at Joint Base Langley-Eustis in Hampton, Virginia, and first started performing in 2007. Typical team size is twenty personnel, including two pilots for two aircraft that are assigned to an air show, with one aircraft flying during the show.

As part of the air show, the F-22 aircraft will fly with older USAF aircraft of the World War II, Korea, and Vietnam eras as part of the heritage flight.

This chapter provides a summary of the major maneuvers that the F-22 demonstration team performs during an air show, along with some of the heritage flight configurations that the F-22 flies in during a show. Maneuvers that are selected for the show depend on weather conditions and cloud ceiling.

Also, some of the special flyover configurations for special events are shown at the end of this chapter, in which the F-22 participates in formation with other aircraft demonstration teams to celebrate special events.

This F-22 Raptor aircraft is preparing for takeoff from Long Island MacArthur Airport in Islip, New York. It is on its way to Jones Beach, located on the south shore of Long Island, some 30 miles away, as part of its participation in the Memorial Day air show. *Ken Neubeck*

Maneuver

The approach if flown from behind the line, approximately 2 miles from show center, with an approximate dive angle of 30 degrees and a maximum of 450-degree cut from the show line. Maintain beyond 500 feet horizontally from the crowd at all times. Upon reaching a point 400 feet from the corner of the crowd at 300 feet AGL, roll the aircraft into a level arching pass, using 75 to 90 degrees of bank. Select full air brakes until passing the show line. Continue the arc until reaching the opposite crowd corner, roll out, reduce power, and initiate a climb.

Used in the High and Low Show

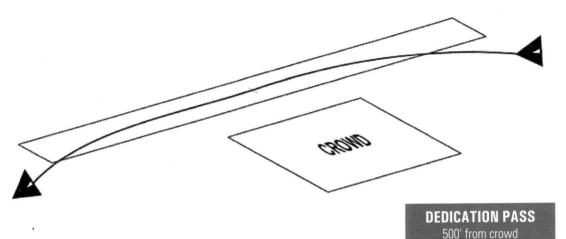

CROWD

DEDICATION PASS
500' from crowd
300' AGL

USAF major Paul Lopez performs the dedication pass during the Spirit of St. Louis Air Show in September 2019. *USAF photo by 2Lt. Sam Eckholm*

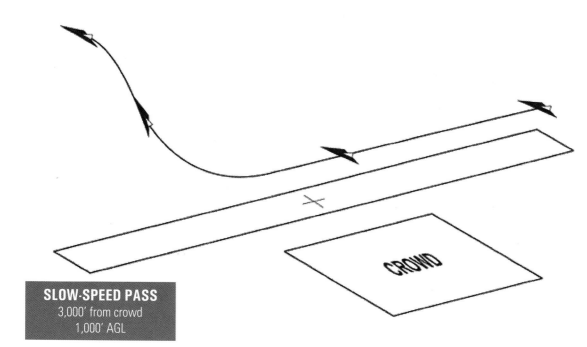

Maneuver

If the wind is negligible or predominantly a crosswind, set the pass to be the same direction as the takeoff. Maintain 120 KCAS (knots calibrated airspeed) in the reposition turn and fly to a point approximately 3,000 feet from the start of the crowd line. Target the line 90 degrees off pass, heading at 1,000 feet AGL and 150 KCAS.

Used in the High and Low Show

SLOW-SPEED PASS
3,000' from crowd
1,000' AGL

CROWD

This F-22 Raptor is performing a slow-speed pass during the practice round of the New York State Air Show in Montgomery, New York, in August 2020. *Ken Neubeck.*

Maneuver

The high-speed pass is flown on the 500-foot show line at 300 feet AGL in maximum power, with a target speed of 0.8 to 0.94 Mach conducted with the aircraft at straight and level flight.

Used in the High and Low Show

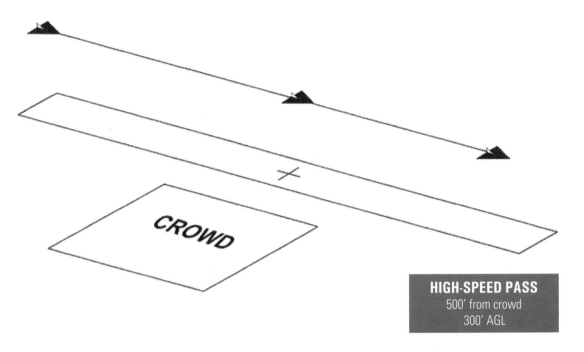

HIGH-SPEED PASS
500' from crowd
300' AGL

US Air Force major Josh Gunderson, F-22 Demo Team pilot and commander, performs the high-speed pass during the Wings Over Houston Airshow, October 10, 2021, at Ellington Airport, Houston, Texas. *USAF photo by SSgt. Donald Hudson*

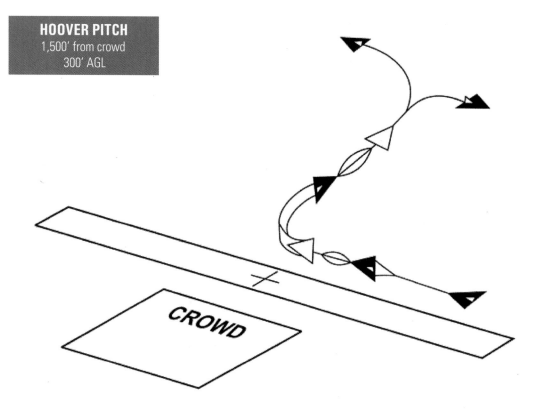

CROWD

Maneuver

The Hoover pitch is flown at the 1,500-foot crowd line at 300 to 400 feet AGL at 300 KCAS. At 3,000 feet prior to show center, the nose of the aircraft is brought up to approximately 5 degrees nose high to obtain 500 feet AGL. When 1,000 feet prior to show center is reached, select full afterburner and roll the aircraft to 90 degrees of bank with the canopy to the crowd. At show center, execute a 190-degree roll into the crowd to establish 80 degrees of bank away from the crowd.

Used in the High and Low Show

US Air Force major Josh Gunderson, F-22 Demo Team commander, performs a Hoover pitch during the Oregon International Air Show on July 31, 2021, in McMinnville, Oregon. *USAF photo by SSgt. Donald Hudson*

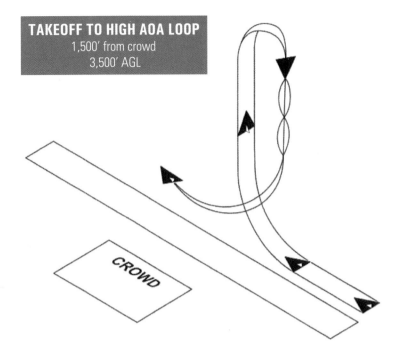

CROWD

Maneuver

Accelerate in full AB with a positive climb rate until approaching show center and on the 1,500-foot show line. At 250 KCAS, begin an aggressive pull up to 75 degrees nose high. Hold 75 degrees nose high and allow airspeed to slow, AOA (angle of attack) to decrease, and altitude to increase. Passing 3,000 feet AGL, smoothly bring the nose to 90 degrees nose high and wait for 3,500 AGI. At 3,500 feet AGL, execute a full-aft-stick high AOA loop to bring the nose to 90 degrees nose low. Hold 90 degrees nose low and accelerate. At 100 KCAS, execute a 405-degree roll to se the lift vector on a 45-degree reposition line. Execute a 36-degree AOA recovery, no lower than 2,000 feet AGL.

Used in the High Show

An F-22 Raptor piloted by a member of the Air Combat Command F-22 demonstration team performs a takeoff to high AOA loop at the Arctic Thunder Open House at Joint Base Elmendorf-Richardson, Alaska, in June 2018. *USAF photo by Alejandro Peña*

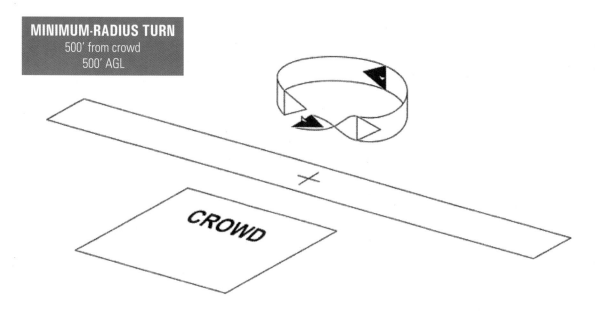

MINIMUM-RADIUS TURN
500' from crowd
500' AGL

CROWD

Maneuver

Beyond the 500-foot show line and at show center, turn away from the crowd, using 75 to 85 degrees of bank. Begin the turn with an aggressive g onset rate to 7.5 g to accelerating and begin bleeding airspeed. G-loading and airspeed bleed-off rate vary with density altitude. The first 180 degrees of turn should be accomplished with a 1¾-degree nose-up attitude, and the last 180 degrees of turn should be accomplished with 1¾-degree nose-down attitude to make the turn appear level to the crowd. As the aircraft approaches show center, smoothly roll out and aggressively pull the nose to 90 degrees nose high.

Used in the High Show

F-22 pilot performs a minimum-radius turn during the F-22 Raptor demonstration at the Battle Creek (Michigan) Field of Flight air show in July 2021. *USAF*

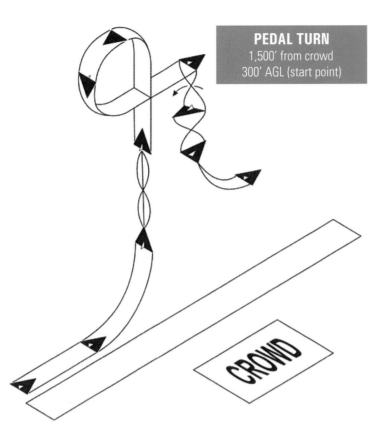

Maneuver

At 1,500-foot crowd line at 300 feet AGL and 300 KCAS, approach show center at full air brake and begin an aggressive pull to 90 degrees nose high. When established 90 degrees nose high with AOA less than 10 degrees, execute a 360-degree roll. Climb and decelerate to arrive at 4,000 feet AGL with no less than 75 KCAS. Execute a maximum wings-level pull to bring the nose through the inverted around to the horizon. As the nose approaches the horizon upright, apply full pedal in the best direction for wings and maintain full-aft stick. Continue the turn for 360 degrees or until lined up at the 1,500-foot crowd line, and begin an aggressive push forward to break the alpha and accelerate. Catch 36 alpha in full air brake mode and arrest the descent rate.

Used in the High Show

An F-22 Raptor performs the pedal turn maneuver at Columbus Air Force Base, Mississippi, in January 2021. *USAF photo by A1C Davis Donaldson*

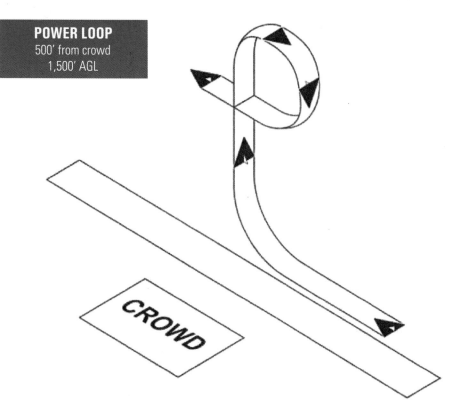

CROWD

Maneuver

Arrive at show center at 1,500 feet AGL and 250 KCAS. Abeam show center, execute a maximum wings-level pull to bring the nose of the aircraft into the vertical. Continue a maximum pull all the way around until the nose of the aircraft is upright and at the starting horizon. Command forward stick to decrease alpha and accelerate. Catch 36 degrees alpha and maintain until sink rate is arrested.

Used in the High Show

Maj. Josh Gunderson, F-22 Raptor demonstration team commander, executes a "power loop" during a performance at Joint Base Elmendorf-Richardson, Alaska, in July 2020. The maneuver uses thrust-vectoring technology unique to the F-22, which allows it to rotate through the air. *USAF photo by 1Lt. Sam Eckholm*

Maneuver

Conduct a high-speed pass and allow the aircraft to reach 4,000 feet AGL and allow the aircraft to accelerate. At 4,000 feet AGL, roll the aircraft inverted and execute an energy-gaining turn to proceed back toward the show center while not exceeding 350 KCAS.

Used in the High Show

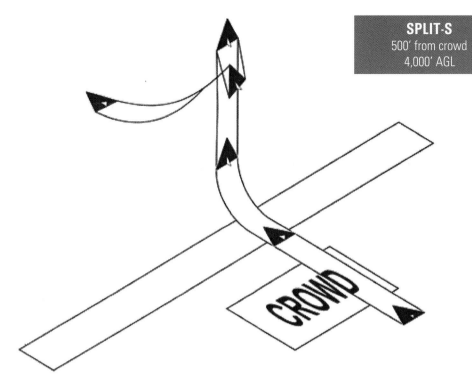

SPLIT-S
500' from crowd
4,000' AGL

Maj. Josh Gunderson, F-22 Raptor demonstration team commander, has the aircraft in inverted position as part of a split-S maneuver during a performance at the Oregon International Airshow in July 2021. *USAF photo by SSgt Daniel Hudson*

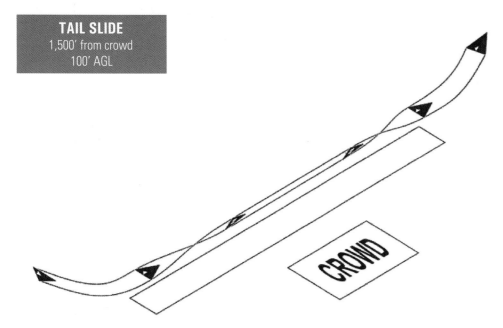

CROWD

Maneuver

Fly over show center at 1,000 AGL and 250 KCAS. At the 1,500-foot show line, execute a hard stop pull to 80 degrees nose high. Hold 80 degrees nose high with back stick pressure and attempt to align the waterline and CDM as the aircraft slows. Modulate power to arrive at 3,000 feet AGL and 0 KCAS. Smoothly reselect maximum power and allow the aircraft so slide backward while holding 80 degrees nose high. At 2,700 feet AGL or 75 KCAS backward, push forward of the soft stop to assist the FLCS in bringing the nose down and reducing AOA. Recover and go to maximum power at wings-level flight.

Used in the High Show

USAF major Paul Lopez, F-22 Demo Team commander, performs the tail slide maneuver during an aerial demonstration at the SkyFest air show in Spokane, Washington, in June 2019. *USAF photo by 2Lt. Samuel Eckholm*

Maneuver

On extended show line, establish wings level and 200 KCAS. Approaching the 500-foot show line, bank away from the crowd, open all doors, and begin a gentle turn to maintain bank, airspeed, and altitude. Passing show center, close all doors, add power, and fly to the 1,500-foot show line.

Used in the High Show

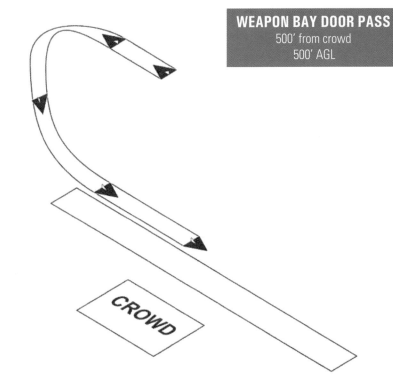

WEAPON BAY DOOR PASS
500' from crowd
500' AGL

CROWD

An F-22 Raptor displays its center and side weapons bays during the weapons bay door pass to the crowd in September 2008, during NAS Oceana Open House. *USAF photo by Edward I. Fagg*

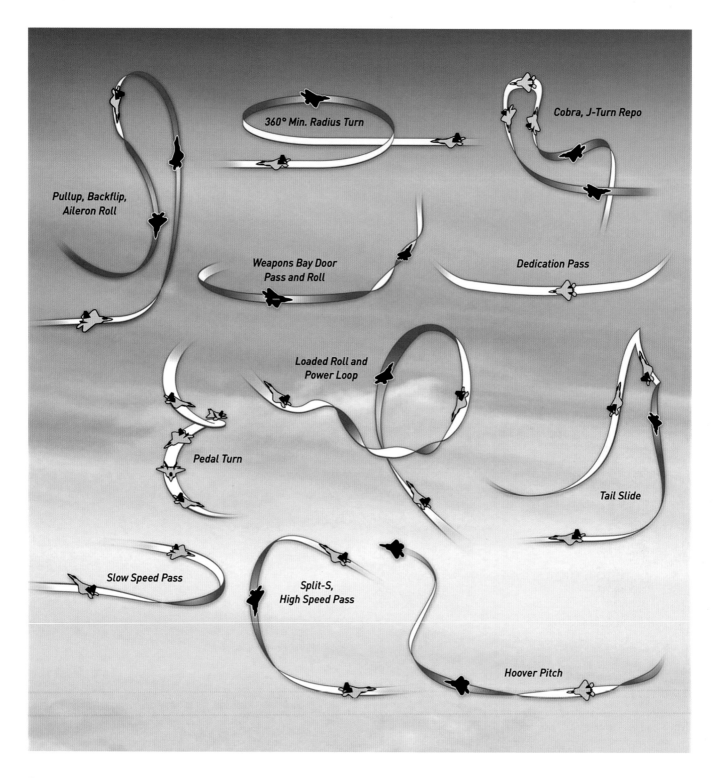

The pictorial shown above summarizes the various F-22 maneuvers that were discussed in this chapter. *USAF*

The F-22 would be a regular participant of the USAF Heritage Flight that is conducted at air shows. Here is an F-22, along with F-4, F-15, and P-51 aircraft, during the Andrews AFB air show in May 2008. *USAF photo by A1C Melissa Rodrigues*

This emblem is on the side of the F-22 demonstration support trailer and shows the F-22, F-35, A-10, F-16, and F-86 aircraft. *Ken Neubeck*

An F-22 Raptor rides behind an A-10C Warthog, with F-35 and F-86 aircraft located on the sides during a heritage flight conducted during the Davis-Monthan air show in March 2019. *USAF photo by 2Lt. Samuel Eckholm*

In August 2019, the F-22 Raptor demonstration team joined with the F-35A Lightning II demonstration team to join with the USAF Thunderbirds and the Royal Air Force Red Arrows team going down the Hudson River in New York to fly past the Statue of Liberty during a promotional visit to New York City in August 2019. The nine aircraft Red Arrows are in a delta formation, with the F-22 and F-35 following in a diamond formation (with the F-22 on the outside part of the diamond). *Ken Neubeck*

In the return flight from the Statue of Liberty, the F-22 and the F-35A teams maintain the same diamond formation going north on the Hudson River, with the F-22 on the outside part. *Ken Neubeck*

An F-22 Raptor from the F-22 demonstration team is seen here in these two photos doing a unique photo opportunity with the Blue Angels during the Marine Corps Air Station air show in Beaufort, South Carolina, in April 2019. The top photo features the F-22 with the six-aircraft Blue Angels formation, and the bottom features the Raptor with the four-aircraft formation of the Blue Angels. *USAF photo by 2Lt. Samuel Eckholm*

Both the F-22 and the F-35 aircraft are fielded by the US Air Force and have similar appearances in shape when in flight, which may be confusing when viewed from the ground. In this side-by-side view of the two aircraft during the practice round of the 2020 New York State Air Show, the F-22A (*top*) can be seen as the larger aircraft compared to the F-35A (*bottom*). The F-22 has a wing section area of 840 square feet, while the F-35 has a wing section area of 460 square feet. The F-22 is also 12 feet longer than the F-35, with a larger wing section area at 840 square feet compared to the F-35A (*shown on bottom*), which has a 460-square-foot area. *Ken Neubeck*

In another view of the two aircraft flying together, with the F-35A on top and the F-22 located below, it can be seen that the F-35A has a single engine exhaust section and the F-22A has a dual engine exhaust section. The F-22A can reach speeds of Mach 2.2, whereas the F-35A can reach speeds of Mach 1.6. *Ken Neubeck*

A lone F-22 from the demonstration team follows a formation of six Thunderbirds F-16 aircraft over Lake Michigan in June 2019. *USAF photo by SSgt. Cory W. Bush*

During training held at Davis-Monthan AFB in Tucson, Arizona, in March 2019, F-22, F-35A, and F-16 aircraft are flying elements of the heritage flight maneuvers in preparation for the upcoming air show season. *USAF photo by Jensen Stidham*

CHAPTER 8
The F-22 Raptor Future

F-22 Raptors wait on the tarmac of MacArthur Airport on Long Island, New York, in May 2022.
Ken Neubeck

Of the original 187 F-22 production aircraft that were built, over 180 remain in service. There is currently no program in place for replacing the Raptor in US Air Force service, although the aircraft will continue to see equipment upgrades in the future.

The F-22 remains active in current events. On February 4, 2023, a surveillance spy balloon that originated from China was spotted at high altitude over the western United States. A few days later, it was deemed safe enough for the balloon to be shot down off the coast of South Carolina, over the Atlantic Ocean. A single F-22 Raptor was dispatched from Langley AFB to fire a sidewinder missile to take down the balloon.

It is important to note that the F-35 JSF Aircraft program is not meant to be a replacement for the F-22 Raptor and the air-superiority role that it maintains, so expect to see the F-22 remain in US service for decades to come.

The F-22 is a critical part of the United States defense since it remains in its role as a deterrent to enemy fighter aircraft as well as an interceptor in its NORAD assignments in northern Alaska. The presence of the F-22 Raptor in the US Air Force is an important role, and it has been fortunate that there has been no conflict in recent years where there was air-to-air combat.

On a yearly basis, the F-22 Raptor demonstration team will have aircraft assigned from either Langley or Tyndall to participate in various air shows held throughout the United States. Here is the team at the New York State Air Show, which was held at Stewart Airport in August 2015. *Ken Neubeck*

For the 2020 New York State Air Show, which was held at Orange County Airport, the F-22 Raptor demonstration team would practice with the F-35A Lightning II demonstration team. The F-22 Raptor is the larger aircraft on the right in this photo. *Ken Neubeck*

Maintenance personnel prepare two F-22 Raptors with F-35C Lightning II aircraft located between them after completion of Jones Beach Air Show participation in May 2022. The F-22 flew to their next scheduled air show demonstration in upstate New York. *Ken Neubeck*

The distinct angled tail sections can be seen for two F-22 Raptors from Langley-Eustis AFB taxiing on the runway of Long Island MacArthur Airport. Two F-22 Raptors are sent to each air show during their demonstration season, even though only one of the aircraft will actually fly each day of the air show. *Ken Neubeck*

This F-22 Raptor is in alert hangar during nighttime training operations conducted at Langley-Eustis AFB in Virginia in February 2019. *US Air National Guard photo by SA Bryan Myhr*

F-22 Raptor is conducting a high-speed pass over a simulated ground explosion of 1,000 feet of flame during the Mission over Malmstrom event that was conducted during the open house at Great Falls, Montana, in July 2019. *USAF photo by Lt. Samuel Eckholm*

This vivid photo is of an F-22 during aerial refueling by a KC-135 during nighttime training operations over the Nevada desert in June 2016. The starboard and port lights on the wings of the aircraft can be seen, along with lighting around the aerial-refueling port on the top of the F-22 aircraft. *USAF photo by A1C Kevin Tanerbaum*